Despite Of!

A Story of Physical, Verbal, and Emotional Abuse

Wayne De-Langè Morris

Dedication

I would like to dedicate this book to my father, James W. Nixon, for teaching me about life and my Mom Mom for always having my back no matter what.

Acknowledgments

My wife for loving me unconditionally and accepting me—flaws and all!

My mother for always showing me love and teaching me how to hustle!

My kids for making me man up when they were born!

About the Author

Wayne D. Morris overcame abuse from his father as a child to become a loving father, husband, businessman, and overall good human being.

Preference: To only be around people who have good energy and who are positive-thinking, get-money people!

Contents

Chapter 1

Life, as I knew it, started on the East side of Hill Creek on the 26th of May 1976. Born to a single mother, Pamela Ann Morris, I grew up thinking that the man we saw around often at our place was my father. He was the first person to take me to the basketball courts and spend time with me as a father would. So, it only made sense that I thought of him as my father despite the fact that he didn't live with us.

I used to call him Dad until I turned five, and my younger sister was born. Her birth brought along a revelation that slightly altered my perception. My supposed Dad took me aside and told me that he was not my father, a truth my mother confirmed as well. He broke it down to me gently that he was my sister's father, not mine, as I already had a father whom I hadn't yet met.

Therefore, I, Wayne De-Langè Morris, harbored a strong desire to meet my biological father, as earlier, I didn't even know his name, what he looked like, or where he lived. That lack of information about him made me curious to find out more.

He was like a blank canvas, allowing me to imagine any face I wanted until the day I would finally meet him in person. All I knew back then was that, unlike other families, my mother was living her life with her children, and he was living his own life somewhere in the same town we lived in Growing up, I saw my mother playing both roles—that of a nurturing soul and a provider for us. Sometimes, it made me wonder if things could have been easier for her if Dad had been around. At least, if the version I imagined him to be was true, then yes, things could have been much better. But reality seldom unfolds like a story, as we have no idea what character will appear in the next chapter of our lives.

My life's first chapter, my childhood, started in Hill Creek, a public housing project in Philadelphia, with my mother. My grandmother, whom I lovingly called Mom Mom, lived around the corner, so she was another face we saw very often. Seven years after my younger sister's birth, a younger brother was also added to our family. But the man who had fathered me wasn't a part of our lives until I turned eleven.

Me, My Mom, and My Sister

Me and My Sister

My curiosity would often get the better of me, and I would end up asking my mother about him. Through her tales of the past, I found out that my father's name was James William Nixon, and he was quite the Casanova of his time. My mom met him when she was too young to date him, barely 14, and he was eight years older than her. Tall and handsome, he easily gained the attention of many ladies, including my mother, who described their first meeting as love at first sight.

He lived in the Raymond Rosen Project down North Philly with his devoutly religious mother. She raised him as a single parent, much like my mother and grandmother had done so with their kids. She tried to raise him right, making sure that he attended service regularly and held Jesus in his heart. But he ended up on the same track his father chose to leave his family for: the dwindling paths of womanizing, rashness, and infidelity.

Thus, I found out that my father wasn't anything like I had imagined him to be. He was no superhero showing up to save the day, and he ended up leaving my mother and me, just like his father did to him and his mother. It was a cycle of making mistakes and discarding responsibility, a cycle that I vowed to break. My father had met his father only once, so he never realized the significance of his role in my life. Lacking any memories to associate with his father or the experience of having a healthy familial bond with him, he deprived my childhood of his presence as well. The image of my father, a blank canvas I had imagined in my mind, remained unchanged until I saw him in Hill Creek, and my mother mentioned in passing that he was my biological father. With a face filling up that canvas, I began to notice him around more often, though his presence hardly had any effect on us. He was just like any other person I would see out on the street, a face I remembered but didn't think much about anymore.

One of my earliest memories of him is quite absurd, but I still remember it quite vividly. My mother and I were going for a ride in his car when he pushed my head down. Just a kid back then who could easily get angered, I felt he had no right to do that and threatened him that I would stab him with a knife once we got home. He laughed as if it was quite amusing for him to see a kid threatening him, which made me flare up. I kept true to my word, and when we got home, I fetched a knife from the kitchen and tried to stab him until my mother intervened. He had twisted my arm to make me drop the knife, and my mother yelled at him to let me go. However, he just laughed and called me a *lil crazy motherfucker.*

Years after that incident, an unexpected encounter brought him back into our lives for a considerably longer period than the brief glimpses we were accustomed to. He met my mom on the train once, coincidentally on the day when a Mike Tyson fight was going to be aired. I wasn't there to witness the scene, but I was told she asked him to come over to our house to watch the fight, and they seemingly hit it off again. My mother had been in love with him from the very beginning. Perhaps meeting him after so long had rekindled those feelings. As for me, his return finally allowed me to put a face to his name. A face I had visualized countless times in my head.

From that evening onward, Dad became a familiar face for us as he would visit often, and initially, I was skeptical about the change being brought into our lives. But the more I got to see my father around, I accepted that perhaps it was for the best. It felt like my long-held wish had been granted. I couldn't have been happier.

He moved in with my mother eventually, and for me, my family was finally complete. However, the solution I had once believed would fix everything in my life—my father's presence—turned out to be very different from what my young mind had imagined.

In the beginning, his presence around us was everything I could have imagined. My father was cheerful and energetic when spending time with me, friendly to my mother, and kind to my other siblings. He seemed full of stories and would start narrating one with just a little bit of encouragement, recounting his experiences as a child in Philadelphia. I would listen enraptured to his tales of surviving on the harsh Philly streets and getting beaten up in the neighborhood, which eventually led him to join a gang for protection.

All those stories and his friendly behavior toward me convinced me that I had a great dad. He might not have been present for the early years of my life, but he was making up for it. With him moving in and my youngest brother just being born, Mom decided that we would need a bigger house. So, we shifted to the West side of Hill Creek and had the biggest house in the neighborhood. We were not rich, but we had everything we needed as my mom worked, and to support her and generate income for myself, I also delivered papers for the Daily News.

Life felt like a dream back then, but of course, like every dream, it had to end, and we woke up to a harsh reality. The warmth from those early days faded much sooner than I hoped, and we started seeing shades other than the bright golden of happiness and comfort.

Dad's charismatic personality was nothing more than a façade that started to melt the more he spent time with us. As months passed, we began to see the first warning signs when he started telling us off for the slightest of things, distancing himself from us gradually by staying out for a night at times and asserting his dominance over my mother.

Regular quarrels and persistent arguments created cracks in the picture of our once happy little family that I had idealized in my mind. Dad was always in a terrible mood, and there were times when he yelled at us and called Mom dreadful names.

Too young to understand the reasons behind the altercations, we kept hoping the rough phase would pass and things would go back to the illusion we were living in before. But that never happened. The arguments only got worse with time, and though we never witnessed any sight of physical violence, it was evident that those blowouts were relentless and were not going to end anytime soon. It stumped me how a man who was so different earlier chose to show us the terrible shades of his personality. Sometimes, he didn't even feel like the dad we knew. He was usually on edge. Even the slightest provocation would send him off. He still tried to participate in our lives actively, but I went from longing for these interactions to being anxious about them.

I was unaware of the reason behind his drastic behavioral change until my cousin told me that Dad was a smoker. At first, I thought he said that as a joke only to annoy me, but then I started noticing that my father might be using some substance that was messing up with him. Too young to confront him outright, I only observed and became more cautious of him.

Sometimes, it made me wonder whether living without my father was the right option for us all along. Not all my memories with him were terrible. We had our fair share of bonding times, too, during which he would tell me about his past. But after his drug addiction, our relationship suffered and went down the drain just like the heroin that he used to block out his senses, chasing a brief moment of ecstasy.

Those brief moments of numbing his senses cost us our happiness, peace, and comfort later when he would take out his frustration on us.

All I knew then was that the life I had enjoyed, the peace of returning home and treating that space as a sanctuary, was forever lost—faded into oblivion. Our home was no longer a place to escape the trials and tribulations of life; it became a persistent nightmare due to my father's temperamental behavior. My father's arrival into our lives had shockingly become the primary cause of our once peaceful life turning into a constant warzone between my parents.

Me and My Parents

Chapter 2

Family has always been a complicated concept for me. I had always felt that the word *family* had more meanings than family members in my life. It was multifaceted, just like the people it was made up of.

Initially, I associated family with a normal life: a mother, a father, and their children. But as time passed, my perception of the word changed colors from the bright golden of a hopeful sunrise to the dusky purple of the dark night.

We had a large extended family, but as I grew older, we gradually stopped visiting them regularly and would only see them occasionally. Most of our relatives lived in Mill Creek, West Philly, with the rest residing in Ambler, PA, making it difficult for us to meet up with them frequently. My immediate family had only five constant members: myself, my mother, my two younger siblings (brother and sister), and Mom Mom, who was the heartbeat of the family and lived around the corner from us in the projects.

Me, My Mom Mom, and My Sister

Then there was my sister's father, whose fleeting appearances in our family came and went like the seasons, temporarily changing our lives with their presence but leaving a deep impact. He was my mother's boyfriend when I was young and the only male I interacted with enough to deem him a father figure.

He went to high school with Mom, and that's how they met and got together. They were dating by the time the fog of my infancy cleared, and the puzzle pieces of my understanding began to click together. But then he joined the Air Force right after high school, and we only got to see him when he would return to town on his break.

My early life with my mother and her boyfriend was a serene stream of good memories. Then, my sister was born, and he told me that he wasn't my father, adding another member to the list of fluctuating figures. However, he was never malicious to me for the reason that I was not his child. What I remember from his time with us is all pleasant, or perhaps because I was a kid back then, viewing everything through rose-colored lenses.

He was supposed to marry Mom and take us with him, but that day never came. Instead, we got accustomed to seeing him only once in three to four months when he would be on break from his duties and visit us. He took my sister to the mall, had dinner with her, and then dropped her back home. Our life seemed to be going smoothly, with no obstacles hindering our path. Still, the persistent distance between them eventually made them drift too far apart to rekindle their relationship. They broke up, and my family was back to just myself, my mother, and my younger sister.

The second time I experienced a change in the meaning of our family was when my biological father moved in with us. I was eleven when he moved in, but I had seen him with Mom and in our neighborhood before that.

My bond with my biological father was very different from the fleeting moments I had experienced with Mom's boyfriend earlier. My fondest memories of that time were listening to stories of his childhood, his time in the gang, and his adventures through the different phases of his life.

Dad had always been a restless soul, a man who lived in the moment and had a flair for adventures. As he was part of a gang, he had sold drugs, gotten locked up, and spent most of his time with girls. His life was a fast track of adrenaline and loud music, fueled with a thirst for excitement and endless pursuit of fleeting highs. The time he spent with me was an overdose of sports and racing, as he would play basketball with me and make me watch football. I was a fan of football back in those days; the game was my life. He knew that and would joke around with me about it.

One time, he led me to believe that my favorite football team, the Philadelphia Eagles, was looking for a player. He said if I trained hard enough, I could get on board. Barely thirteen at that time, I believed him, and those training sessions became another source of bonding for us. Even though I realized later that he was only joking about the Eagles recruiting me, I remember all those times that make up the happiest memories from my childhood.

I also remember the road trip to New York to visit my grandfather. It marked another happy but distant memory of childhood when my father took us to amusement parks, got involved in our lives positively, and seemed to support our family strongly.

Little did I know that the version of him I found so endearing was his euphoric state when he was high. I was too young to understand back then, and my mom was also unaware of his addiction until they got married a few years later.

The cracks in the ecstatic image of my father began to form when he would not be high. Mom and I began noticing the warning signs when his mood started to shift. From the always happy and enthusiastic man, he would abruptly turn into a mean bully. In that contrasting shade of his personality, he would become a menace to be around, nothing like the man I had come to know him as in the past few months.

My mother figured out the reason behind his snappy behavior, which was causing constant rifts between them. She got stuck in a terrible situation as she couldn't expose his addiction because then she would get blamed for marrying a man who was already on the road to destruction. Each time she confronted him, it ended in a massive fight, a screaming match that terrified my younger siblings and kept me awake all night, wondering what turn would change the path laid out in front of our family.

Mom didn't tell us about his addiction either, nor why he was a paradox of feelings, cheerful one moment and rude the next. We had no idea what made him unstable until my cousin mentioned in passing that Dad was a smoker. Later on, I learned how he got hooked on heroin when he was once telling me about his time selling drugs.

He had an innate fear of needles and anything to do with hospitals. Thus, he stayed away from injecting drugs into his bloodstream initially. He would sell drugs and watch his friends shoot themselves up with heroin. The euphoria they experienced as a result would fascinate him, but his fear of needles kept him at bay. He told me the first time he tried heroin was when he saw his friend snorting it. Realizing that there were other ways to consume that drug, he began pestering his friend to give him some heroin to try out. At first, his friend refused, saying, "It's not for you, Nick. You will regret doing it." But after he kept bothering him, he gave him some of that deadly powder to snort. No needles, no fear, and that freedom that gripped him after snorting the powdery substance got my dad hooked on heroin.

It happened way before he became a significant part of our lives, so when we met him, we had no idea that we were interacting with the goofy and amiable façade that engulfed him only when he was high. Constantly consuming the drug kept him satiated, and we were also happy because he spent time with us, played basketball, and raced with me through the neighborhood. He was the best version of himself when he was high, floating on a cloud that kept the dark side of his personality locked out of sight.

While his euphoria was inflicted by drugs, my euphoria was inflicted by finally having a father who I hoped would stay with us forever. Little did I know back then that hope would shatter, and its shards would make us bleed profusely.

The happiness I felt with my father was soon clouded by his unexpected mood swings. Whenever he was running short of heroin, the other side of his personality came to the surface, which was totally opposite from the man we had grown fond of. I don't even recall when the first time he treated me awfully was, as it was so long ago. But then it became a pattern, a patchwork held together by mistakes, punishments, and foul words that eventually escalated to beatings. He never laid a hand on my sister, and he never hit my mother in front of me, but I would often take the brunt of his unstable mood swings. When he was angry and couldn't find the heroin to take him into the world of no accountability, he would take out all his pent-up anger on me.

Sadly, that was how I learned to fight from him. He would stuff my mouth with paper towels and wrap up my arms with dish rags. Then, taking his own dish rag and wrapping it around his fists and using paper towels as a mouth guard, he would hit me, giving me the rough treatment until I stood up and fought back. Perhaps that was how he had been taught to fight back when he was part of the gang. But his fragmented reality made him unable to understand that I was just a child and the way he fought would hurt me.

My body would often be a tapestry of black and purple, proof of how hard his punches got me. It might have taught me resilience, but back then, I knew it was something no other boy my age would be going through. It felt unfair and hurt even worse.

However, those fights in the living room were not the end of the punishments that he inflicted on me. If I ever got bad grades on my report card, he would make me do push-ups and jumping jacks until my body turned sore from all the fatigue. Up until I was sixteen, I kept tolerating that abusive behavior from my father, hoping every day that he would go back to being the awesome Dad he used to be earlier. But for that, he would have to get high again, and it would cause trouble between him and Mom. To avoid the bitter situation at home, I applied for a job at McDonald's. But even then, Dad picked another way to exploit me as he would often show up and ask for money from my mother and I. Mom's fights with him had also gotten worse. Not having any money on himself, he would come and take it from us, not caring if we had to buy something or were saving that money for other purposes.

Whenever he decided to get the money from us, he would not leave until we gave in. I remember how he showed up at the restaurant where I worked and forced me to take a break and then get him some cash. Thus, even if I was working all my shifts to earn some money, it was being used up on cheap thrills as my dad left me no choice but to hand those hard-earned bucks over.

Dad—a word that I associated with fun, past stories, and adventures—became tainted with the murky shades of his addiction, irresponsibility, and withdrawal symptoms. Gradually, the unpleasant side of his personality became a permanent resident in his body, overshadowing the pleasant memories we had with him in the past.

It felt like years had lapsed since those days when life was happy and comfortable, and each time we thought about the past, it felt unattainable—a distant dream that had very soon transitioned into a nightmare.

In all those years, the only thing that kept me sane was a bubble I had formed in my life, filling it up with my love for basketball, my job, and the time I spent with my friends, including girls. In that bubble, Dad's abuse did not exist, and once I was within my zone, I would push out all the regret and bitterness. I don't really know, but perhaps that was how my father had dealt with his problems back when he was young. For me, it was a brief escape to be in my bubble and turn all the locks, detaching myself from the harsh reality that I lived in.

The family I had was dysfunctional due to my father, who was slowly poisoning our lives with his toxic existence. But I pushed myself through those difficult times, getting all the toxicity out of my system eventually in the best way I could.

Chapter 3

I started noticing the difference in my father's behavior after my cousin told me that he smoked drugs.

At first, I didn't know what was the reason behind his fluctuating moods. But then I slowly began to realize that he was a different person entirely when he was high.

The humorous and energetic Dad I knew from my childhood was a result of the drugs he consumed. Whenever he was high, he acted like he had no care in the world, and it seemed as if he was in a bubble of happiness. He didn't get angry; he wouldn't yell at my mother or me, nor would he put his hands on me.

However, those moments were short-lived because once the intoxication wore off, he would desperately search for an escape, becoming violent toward us when he couldn't find his drugs. Another telltale sign of him being high was his detachedness to things around him. He would only focus on playing with his toes and watching movies and would drift off to sleep in the middle of it. Whenever we tried to close the television set, he would wake up and tell us to keep it running, saying that he was watching the movie even though he had been fast asleep seconds earlier.

Thus, he would play the movie from the beginning and go back to his habit of playing with his feet carelessly. Just like the movie playing from the beginning, our lives, too, seemed to have gotten stuck in a monotonous loop that went through the same film over and over again whenever the remote control was in his hands. One time, I went to the bathroom after him and found out that it smelled weird. I couldn't quite figure out what that smell was, but later, I realized that my dad had mixed some cocaine with weed and smoked it. As a result, the bathroom reeked of those heady fumes that I had to exhaust through the small window.

He also looked different whenever he was high. I had only seen him do drugs in front of me once, but I could always tell by the way he looked that he wasn't sober. I had learned to pick up on the small warning signs, the indicators of when I had to be cautious and when I could just let go.

Even though those times were weird, it was still better than the times when he was sober. Without the drugs furnishing him with rose-colored lenses, he turned into nothing short of a monster for us.

At the age when children are afraid of the monsters hiding in the closet or under the bed, I was facing a monster in our home who not only threw insults at us but also resorted to physical abuse.

I knew it wasn't normal and not something other children my age were going through.

Most of my friends didn't have their fathers in their lives. I was one of the few who had someone fulfilling that role. But the physical and verbal abuse I had to go through hardly made me seem any luckier by having a father in my life. True, not all the times were bad, but most of my memories were tainted with the bitterness of his words and the rough impact of his callous hands, the marks of which were often etched on my skin in a patchwork of black and purple.

Fear became a constant companion in my life, a tool that my father used to make me do things I didn't want to. In the middle of the night, I would often be woken up by his gruff voice, demanding money from me, which I would be forced to hand over as I was afraid of what he would do if I didn't comply.

He would storm inside my room, blasting one of his favorite songs, Fuck the Police, by the NWA—a hardcore rap group from Compton, California. That was his usual way of waking me up in the morning.

He also had another habit of checking my room like a correctional officer checks the inmates for contraband or weapons. Just like the CO goes to the cell and rips it apart in his search for compromising items, Dad would act like my correctional officer. He would come into my room, send me out, then tear it all apart and make me clean it up afterward. I was just a kid back then and didn't know why he did that to me or what exactly he was searching for. But now, when I think about it, I guess it was his way of preventing me from going down the route of doing drugs, roaming the streets, going to jail, etc.

Back then, he was much bigger and stronger than me, so I never took the risk of going against his words. I never wanted to give him a reason to beat me up, giving in to his demands even when they were unjust. With my hard-earned money, he would buy more drugs, get high, and return to being the less violent but more detached version of himself. A stark difference existed in the times when Dad was away from home and when he returned. My siblings and I would play around and have fun in his brief absence, but each time we heard his car approaching, it seemed as if the whole house tensed up along with us, waiting for the inevitable.

My room would become a temporary refuge as I would lock the door and wait for Dad to leave again. The anxiety of watching the seconds tick by on the clock while I hoped he wouldn't come up and bother me was a feeling I got accustomed to just because it happened so often.

Growing up in a toxic environment created by my father, I would have suffocated if not for the only outlet I had. My passion for sports became the one place where I could channel all the pain and frustration into something positive.

My first love was football, and it was the first time I felt I could endear myself to a sport passionately and play to the best of my ability. Then, as I started playing basketball, I realized that I loved it more than football. The adrenaline rush, 3-point shots, top-tier defense, and dope layup packages all fueled my experience of the game. It fueled me to move on with my life even though I was being treated like a punching bag at home. Each time I practiced and played the sport, I felt a sense of freedom that I had never had before. With each game, I would push out the hurt building up inside me so that it wouldn't end up making me explode. In a sense, sports became my saving grace. Unable to fight back against the abuse I suffered at home, I began to look for other outlets to feel free and liberated from the chains that bound me otherwise. My dad was using drugs to escape from his life; I used money, basketball, and girls to escape mine.

Call it an inheritance or a need of the time being, I was quite popular with the girls, just like my father. I knew about it, too, and the attention I received from them felt like nothing short of a temporary lock on the monsters of my life spilling out of my mind's closet.

If I hadn't had these brief escapades, I could have easily gone mad from the trauma and the helplessness. Those distractions served their purpose well and prevented my descent into the quagmires of self-degradation.

There were times when I considered getting rid of my father. I might never have stood up to him before that, but I knew the way he treated me was wrong and that I had to stop. I had planned it all out, rehearsing it in my mind that I would go to my friend's and borrow his gun to do the deed and never look back.

It might be easy to think about it, but executing it came with a lot of complications that I didn't want to face. I didn't want to go to jail, and perhaps that knowledge of being sent to do my time in prison kept me from acting out on that plan.

I was so exhausted from being the punching bag for my family that I just wanted it to come to an end. My sister would sometimes complain about me to my mother and get me in trouble. Even when she didn't cause more issues for me, Dad would be waiting to take out all his frustration on me. I was the ball tossed around from one court to another, with the players hardly caring that it caused me to get hurt.

In those trialing times, the only support I had was Mom Mom, with whom I could share the mistreatment I was going through. She always took my side and even tried to tell Mom to stop Dad from hurting us and arguing with her.

Me and My Mom Mom

Sometimes, I felt my mom was scared of me retaliating against Dad, so she never told me about their arguments. She worked long hours as Dad didn't contribute to the household expenses, so most of the time, she would not be at home. The short time she spent at home was also marked with arguments. They fought often but behind closed doors. Later, she said she always took a stand for us and tried to put Dad in his place. But in those days, it felt as if we were thrown into a tempest without a lifeline, whirling in the deep waters until we got swallowed up whole.

I had started working early on in life to handle my own expenses as I knew my mother was already burdened having to bear the weight of her children as well as her husband. Worked double shifts at the Einstein Hospital, which was the same medical facility where I was born. Knowing how hard it was for her to keep our family afloat financially, I told her that she need not worry about me. Thus, from a young age, I bought my own clothes and shoes, hoping it would take some burden off my mother's shoulders.

However, even if I was taking care of my own expenses, it didn't make much difference to the tasks my mother had to look after herself. Dad never shared the responsibilities of running the house, so she always had to manage things on her own. Whatever money Dad made, by either scalping tickets for basketball games or selling drugs, he would spend it all on his own fleeting pleasures. When he needed money for drugs, he would come to me or Mom. If we refused to give him money or didn't have it on us, he would try other means, such as one incident I still remember vividly. He took me to the convenience store, picked some things up, and told me to go to the counter and lie about losing the receipt so that they would give us the money back for those things.

I had no choice but to follow his lead and did as I was told. However, the people at the store realized something was wrong, and even though they didn't say anything to me and even returned money that we hadn't even paid, they called the cops on my dad.

However, no sort of threat could really work on changing his ways, and we found out that rehab wasn't the solution for him, either. Dad had been sent to rehab two to three times while he was living with us, but even that didn't help him. Whenever he returned from rehab, he would be better for a few days before lapsing into his old habits and consuming drugs again.

I realized the terrifying power heroin could have on a man at that time because it would take hold of Dad even after he returned from rehab, making him return to his fluctuating moods and bad habits. Then, from heroin, his habits extended to cocaine and weed that he would smoke or snort. He never injected himself with substances but got high after snorting the fatal powder.

There were times when he made me sell drugs for money. Even though I did it, anxious that I would get beaten up if I refused, the fear of being caught and sent to jail also kept me up at night. Dad had that realization, too, that he shouldn't have involved me in the drug business; he later admitted it himself. But back then, it felt like I was his sidekick, someone he could get to do anything for him, and he used that knowledge to his benefit. Or perhaps it was the drugs clouding his senses that blurred the lines between right and wrong.

Looking back at the time of my life spent with Dad, I can only see a torrent of bad decisions that I was being thrust into by my father. Whether it was merely for the thrill of it, the adrenaline rush, or to measure up to an image of Dad's childhood, he made me do stuff I would never have done so otherwise.

Once, at a basketball game that he was scalping tickets for, he made me work for a newspaper guy for the day. I was tasked to sell newspapers and return the money to the man who would later pay me out of that money. But Dad made me keep all the money I made from selling newspapers even though it was wrong. He told me to give him forty dollars, joking that he made me work to get paid, so I shouldn't have any problem giving some of it to him. Then, he made us board a train so that the newspaper guy wouldn't catch us and then spent that money on cocaine and warned me not to tell Mom about it.

It was the first time he snorted cocaine in front of me, cementing the perception of him doing drugs. I had never seen him use drugs before that day, and right then, seeing him so careless about the money and the way he had snorted it all up, I felt hurt and regret claw at my insides.

Was this the father I had wanted in my life?

Or was he becoming a parasite leaching on us and sucking us dry?

Whatever the case, I hadn't signed up for that kind of life, and I wasn't going to put up with it for long.

I decided not to let those rough tides break my strength. Instead, I looked upon it as a means to get stronger. From my perspective, I was building up my resilience to be able to fight back and break the cycle of torment.

Chapter 4

The seeds of our personality are sown in the fertile ground of childhood experiences. Thus, the person we become is often a result of how we were treated in our younger years, as all those experiences come together to shape us. We think and act a certain way based on our fears, motivations, and impacting factors from childhood.

The same happened with my father.

He grew up to be a self-centered man who constantly chased an illusion due to his childhood that he could never abandon in his past. He wanted to escape from the things that tied him to his past and present. Perhaps that was why he resorted to using drugs as a means of escapism.

Being the youngest in a household full of women, as he lived with his mother and sisters, my dad grew up challenging the people who surrounded him. He subconsciously learned from their lives and absorbed their experiences like a sponge.

He saw his sisters treat their boyfriends badly and cheat on them, which engrained this perception in his mind from a very young age that all women were cheaters. He didn't want to be in the shoes of the men who wooed his sisters and then suffered for it.

So, he decided to never let himself be treated that way by always being the first one to cheat and be insincere. The behaviors he had seen in his past reflected into his present, turning him into a man who could never have a serious relationship because he thought women could never be sincere. It gave him the motivation to not be sincere himself, commit acts of adultery, and defy responsibilities to every extent possible.

His mother once told him that a poor rat only has one hole to crawl back into. He challenged that mindset as well, never settling down to a single home or family. Aside from me and my mother, he had a total of eight children from six other women. But each time things began to get serious, he would break himself off from the confines of that relationship, returning to the streets to find some new thrill to embark on.

He once told me that he only dated women who put up with his carefree lifestyle. Even when he was in a relationship, he would be messing around with other women. Thus, he would never be the provider in the relationship. Instead, he always took what he was given and kept taking more with time. Whether it was also due to his past experience of seeing his sisters receiving gifts from their boyfriends, or it was his own selfishness clouding his sense of responsibility, he simply didn't want to be the one putting in the money and the effort. He stayed with the women until they got tired of all the cheating and the carelessness on his part. Then he would just leave, finding another companion to keep him company. When he first met my mother, he already had two daughters with two different women, then another daughter with the woman he ended up marrying at

21. He went on to have three children with his wife. But that didn't stop him from cheating on her, and after the second child, who was a son and a year older than me, he cheated on her with my mom and had me. After my birth, he had a third child with his wife, but eventually, she got tired of all the cheating and kicked him out of the house.

He met my mother again after his wife had kicked him out of the house and probably divorced him. It was another chance for him, perhaps, and he got together with my mom, marrying her when I was about twelve or thirteen years old. But soon enough, my mom realized that he wasn't the man she wanted to spend the rest of her life with.

My dad had a job before he settled down with my mom. He used to work for the Philadelphia School District in food services during the day. After he got together with Mom and joined our family, he found a night job for housekeeping at the Naval base that started around seven in the evening, four hours after he got free from his first job.

In those four hours, he would spend his time on the streets, hanging out with his friends and getting high. He also hacked, meaning he offered to drop people from one place to another in his car for a cheaper fare than cabs.

Thus, he met all sorts of people and hung out in the city in the time he had before going to his other job. That habit of his didn't change after meeting Mom. The only difference was that he had moved in with us and shared our roof. I remember that he used to make me and my siblings clean the house sometimes. I was thirteen or fourteen years old back then and can recall the events as clearly as if it was just yesterday. He would tell us to clean and sweep the house using a mop. We did it to the best of our ability, mopping everything until no specks of dust could be seen.

However, my dad had a strange way of checking if things were completely clean or not. He would wear a white glove and rub it on the counters, the floors, and the woodwork to check if the white fabric got stained with any dust we could have left behind. Thus, he made us clean everything over and over again, finding amusement in our struggles. I found out later that it was how he was checked by the chef at his work.

The chef wore a white glove to check the surfaces of the kitchen and would make my dad clean them again if he missed anything. So, his telling us to clean the house and check it in the same way was a reenactment of what he went through at work.

However, he never missed a day of work and earned from his jobs, sometimes giving the money to my mother on Fridays to look after the bills and other expenses. But, sometimes, he would ask her to give it back to him on Sundays, and when she refused, he would get upset.

My mother had been putting up with his behavior and raising us at the same time while being a working woman herself. She worked at the hospital, where she completed double shifts and had side hustles to provide for us. She had too much on her plate to notice that Dad was going behind her back and cheating on her. I feel that she should have known about the other women in Dad's life, considering that he had been a ladies' man even before he met her. But when I asked her about it later, she said she had no idea about his infidelity. For him, being with one woman and still having fun with others was no new thing.

Perhaps he had thought the time would come soon for Mom to abandon him as well, and he needed another temporary shelter. His childhood molded him into being selfish and always prioritizing his own needs. So, the other women he saw were kind of his backup in case the crumbling family he had with my mother refused to bear his weight any longer.

He didn't want to be a poor rat with only one house to crawl into. He wanted to prove his mother wrong and keep his options open. Thus, he had eight children altogether, and I got to meet them all over the course of time that my dad lived with us. My older brother came to live with us when I was in high school. We have photographs and shared memories of the time we hung out with each other. I only had one sister who I didn't meet with back then and was only able to meet a few years earlier from now.

Just like the childhood that he experienced shaped my father, the childhood he gave me shaped me to become the man I am today.

I grew up observing him and being influenced by the rough methods he taught me to deal with my life. Even when he tried to help me with my homework or taught me how to fight, he made sure that it would rough me up. Perhaps he had subconsciously learned that to survive, one needed to be tough, and to be tough, one needed to experience hardships. Each time I spent with him became a mark on my personality, shaping me in ways no other factors could. He was transferring his experiences to me through his methods of teaching me to fight and threatening to beat me up if I did my homework wrong. Thus, my childhood became a chain of negative reinforcement from my father. I grew up hating him for being a source of discomfort to our family, but it also taught me that I should never act that way with my own children and partner.

It taught me that I had to be loyal, take care of my responsibilities, and never treat my children the way my father treated me. Years later, when I was old enough to come to terms with my past, and my father felt remorse for his actions, he asked me to forgive him, which I did. After that, we were able to work on our relationship positively, but it didn't change the years of hurt that tainted my childhood and early adolescent years. I forgave him, but I never forgot.

In a sense, Dad became a living example of all I had to avoid doing in my life so that my family wouldn't be affected as adversely as I had been under his mentorship.

Chapter 5

Recalling my childhood and young adult years, I am reminded of how my parents influenced my life deeply. On the one hand, was my father, with whom I had a complex relationship, and on the other was my mother, who was burdened with the responsibilities of raising us.

My dad was the type of guy who would get angry very easily, and then he would raise his voice, and his eyes would go big. When he got angry, he didn't care what words came out of his mouth, so he would say a lot of things that would end up hurting other people. I had been an audience and a victim of his anger several times, so I had seen it all firsthand.

He wasn't a very muscular guy, the type you see in movies who gets angry and makes others scared by how intimidating they look. My dad was always skinny, but his loud voice and painful words contributed to making him seem just as intimidating. In his anger, he would talk harshly to my mother, too, and call her names; each word of it is ingrained in my memory. And it terrified me further that if I did anything to anger him, he could treat me even worse.

When I was younger, I would mostly mind my business and never got in between my mom and dad's arguments. While the fear of confronting my father's anger and beatings was very real, I refused to let it paralyze me. I shouldered the burden in silence, determined not to burden my already busy mother. However, I would sometimes think that she should have taken a stand for me. We lived under the same roof, and even if she wasn't home a lot due to her job and side hustles, she knew I was being used as a punching bag by my father to take out all his pent-up frustration. She knew, but she did nothing to warn him or kick him out of the house because he was hurting her son. That realization made me feel I couldn't go to my mother and tell her about the abuse because she would do nothing.

My mother told me later that she and my dad had often gotten into arguments about the way he treated me. She said she tried to stop him from abusing me and fought with him for that, even though it never happened in front of me. Behind closed doors, my mom and dad were arguing about me, and she wanted to protect me. But back then, I didn't see any effort from her side, so I had to seek help from the only other person I could contact.

When the beatings got worse, I went to Mom Mom. I felt my mom was too busy with her work to care for me, and Dad would never stop taking out his anger on me. So, in those times, Mom Mom was my only hope.

When I told her about the abuse, she reprimanded my mom for not taking a stand for me, and she kicked her out of her house. In return, my mom had an argument with Dad over his behavior, which resulted in another beating for me. My dad didn't like that I told her about how he treated me in the house, and he took it all out on me again. He said that whatever happened in the house should stay in the house, and I should not have told any outsider about it. But what else could I do? From the age of eleven and up until sixteen, I was taking the brunt of his aggression. I had to confide in someone I could trust, but eventually, I stopped telling Mom Mom, too, because all it got me was another beating.

In those trialing circumstances, I found respite in the times when I was not at home to witness the messed-up family drama I was living in. I did not like attending school, but it gave me the opportunity to leave the bitterness of life and channel it through other outlets. From a young age, I had always been good at sports. We lived in a project, and all the children in my neighborhood would play outside. We played tackle football on the grass, and we even played basketball and baseball.

That early exposure to sports and my potential to perform well in each game furnished me with my escapism. When I was out there playing to my heart's content, I didn't have to think about my father's abuse and my mother's silence over his actions. So, I kept playing, and sports became a significant aspect of my life.

I remember winning a football championship when I was thirteen years old. I played for the Olney Eagles, and it was my first experience to go through the selection process and prove myself worthy to make it to the team. The selection process was fierce, but I wasn't intimidated by the competition. We trained hard, pushing ourselves to the limit, and the cuts were brutal. But I didn't back down. I earned my spot and didn't just play—we dominated, securing the championship title. I had yet to go to high school, but that win ignited a fire in me. I knew I could compete well, and I was hungry for more. Thus, I set my eyes on trying out for the high school sports teams as well.

Dominating the court wasn't just a one-time thing. I took my talents to the Tabor Rams, where I quickly established myself as the team's star player. Polishing those skills became my obsession, and when I reached high school, basketball was a natural choice.

There, I discovered my true calling, a place where I could truly shine. I was a 3 and D player—a silky smooth left-handed player who could shoot with the best of them fearlessly.

Aside from playing sports with the neighborhood children, I also had side hustles to support my mom and look after my needs. I was the oldest of her children, and I wanted to share her responsibilities so that it would be easier for her to raise us. From a young age, I told her not to worry about me, and when I was eleven, I delivered papers to save some money for my stationery items and other school supplies. Getting older, I started working at the Hoagie store with my mother. I learned to do several different tasks there and realized firsthand that earning money wasn't easy. I got paid every Saturday for my job, and they made me do all sorts of tasks, from taking out the trash to cutting meat and onions.

The money I earned there was enough for me to handle my necessities. I could go and get a haircut and save money to buy anything I needed for school or sports. I was fourteen when I left the Hoagie store and sought a job at McDonald's in the summer before high school. I worked at the restaurant till tenth grade, and then I quit. Leaving my neighborhood elementary school, I joined Samuel Fels High School in 1991, and life took a turn from there. I was the only boy from my project who attended Fels High that year. My upbeat personality and talent in sports landed me a place with the cool kids, and I remember being quite popular in high school.

However, basketball and football weren't the only fields where my talents were appreciated at that time. Being handsome and a people person, I was popular with the girls, too. Call it an inherent trait of my father's or just picking it up from the environment I grew up in as I was a cool dude from the hood, I became quite a ladies' man myself. My dad used to say we were handsome dudes who didn't need corny pickup lines to get together with girls. I saw what he meant when I started high school and became the center of attention.

High school wasn't a refuge for me; it was a battlefield I conquered. Sure, my home life was a mess, but I wasn't going to let that define me at school. Most of my peers never suspected anything about my abusive home life, as I was always cheerful and outgoing. Sports and friendships became my weapons, and I flourished in the adrenaline-driven environment.

Another significant aspect of my personality was my conversation skills. I grew up in a neighborhood that was mainly black to white, but I had attended cultural schools where I interacted with a diverse community. My classmates were American but had roots in China, Russia, France, and other parts of the world. So, I was always open to being paired up with people of different races and ethnicities. If you put me in a room with a diverse group of people, I would easily converse with them and befriend them.

I liked to build people up by complimenting them and making them feel good about themselves. If I saw someone wearing a nice pair of sneakers or a cool hairstyle, I would tell them that it looks good on them.

I never got bullied in high school. However, I can recall an incident from my early years when I was bullied, and I stood up for myself.

I was killing time, just chilling with my friends from another neighborhood. It was then this older guy sauntered up to us—he was three or four years older than me, and we knew each other as he was from my project. We played and fought together like brothers, so I mostly didn't mind what he said.

That day, I could tell the dude was a little buzzed, as he had this cocky swagger when he approached me. He said, "What's up, Boody? Let's slap box."

I wasn't in the mood right then, so I refused, "No, I don't wanna slap box, go ahead." He asked me again, and when I still didn't agree, he reared back and slapped me in the face, right there in front of my boys. In that moment, I saw red.

First of all, you don't smack no man. You don't smack no man in the face, period. But he slapped me in front of my two homies that didn't live around here. They came to the project with me. So, I jumped up and hit him hard, knocking him to the ground.

If I didn't stand up for myself and did nothing at that time, I'd have been known as a pussy, and my homies would have been looking at me funny. My name would have been like trash in the project, so I had to do something.

I hit him across the head, his face, his body—just messing him up. The dude had caught me by surprise with that slap, but now I was letting out all my rage on him.

I was so hyped then that I just took off, needing to walk it off before I did something I'd regret. So, I walked off, and when I came back after half an hour, my boys told me that after I left, that guy had gone and convinced an older guy to give him a gun.

The older guy must have been drinking and not thinking straight as he just handed the guy a gun, and then he was out there swinging it around, looking for me. He came up to my friends, too, asking for me and waving the gun in front of them. He said, "Where are y'all Boody fans at?"

But I wasn't there, so he left by the time I got back around the corner. My friends told me what happened, and I never had any problems after that. But after that day, I never had a problem with him again and wasn't bullied. He knew if he did anything to disrespect me, I would fight back and not back down because my Dad had taught me well. So, I had a close call that day, and if he had encountered me with that gun, perhaps I wouldn't have been here to tell the tale. But that incident taught me a lot.

I was never scared of anyone after that because I knew I could take them on. Thus, it was one instance in which I could genuinely say that my father's attempts to make me tough to face the world ended up helping me. Even though I was left broken and bruised by the end of the fights with my dad, all those hours of taking him on made me learn how to fight and not be scared anymore.

That early experience with bullying solidified a principle for life: I wouldn't tolerate disrespect, and I wouldn't dish it out, either. It wasn't about avoiding trouble; it was about setting boundaries and navigating the world with integrity. My path was clear—to be a force for good, a law-abiding citizen who contributes positively to society. In all the years past, I never stepped foot inside a jail and never ended up in a situation where I would get reprimanded. I guess I had had enough beatings to last me a lifetime, and I steered clear of any other instances where I could get myself in trouble.

I surrounded myself with the best people, just like I used to do when I was younger. You must have heard the saying that a man is known by the company he keeps. I embraced that saying entirely and ensured that my company was worth being proud of. A tough childhood could have easily defined me, but I refused to let it dictate my future. Instead, I took charge and built a network of friends and mentors who inspired and uplifted me. Feeling alone throughout my childhood, I wanted my later years to be the best, surrounded by good people and having the best time of my life. So, in my own way, I tried to make it happen first through sports and then through finding friends and spending time with girls. I crafted my own company and ensured that it would be the best, so I wouldn't have to think about the abuse I was suffering at home.

Chapter 6

Just like my dad influenced my life and childhood through his behavior, I must mention my mom, who had an equally significant but opposite impact on me. She was a positive influence on me, and from the start, she made sure that her children were taken care of, even if that meant working hard and not getting any rest for herself.

Me and My Mom

One of my cherished memories with her is going to the market to buy lunch meat and potato chips. We would eat lunch meat with juice and soda, which felt like a special treat. Later, when I was older, mom told me that she didn't have enough money, so she only bought lunch meat, and we would often have them for dinner as well. However, being young children unaware of the harsh realities of the world, we easily cherished what we got and made the best out of it.

All my memories of early life, which were tainted with Dad's verbal and physical abuse, also include my mom, who was trying her best to look out for us and make ends meet. She spent eight years in marriage with a man who was a heroin addict, only because she was unaware of his addiction earlier. When she found out, she was already on her honeymoon and was scared of what people would say if she left him.

Thus, she spent eight years living with a man who could scare her with his temper and who beat up his own son in an attempt to make him tougher. The only thing I held against her was why she let me get abused by Dad when she knew I was suffering. She loved me and cared for me, I have no doubt about that, but she still didn't stop Dad from using me as a literal and metaphorical punching bag.

I remember going through two incidents when my dad got so rough with us that my mom had to take her children and leave the house to stay away from him. The first time it happened, she took us to her friend's house, and we stayed there for a few weeks. The other time, when Dad got terribly angry, Mom Mom told us to come over to her place, so Mom gathered all our things and went to her mother's house. The threat subsided for the time being until my father came up to her place, intending to talk to my mother and convince her to return home. She refused to let him in until he insisted and said he only wanted to talk to her daughter. I remember the events of that night as afresh as if they happened just yesterday.

Dad came inside to talk, and I was in the living room while they were talking. Mom Mom left to give them privacy, and that was when things escalated. Dad and Mom's discussion soon became an argument, and when he got aggressive and tried to put his hands on my mom, Mom Mom pulled out her gun at him.

It was an impactful sight, seeing her pull out a gun on Dad to protect Mom. However, he also pulled out a gun on her, and with firearms pointing at one another, the argument resumed. My mother came in between them, holding her hands up and trying to diffuse the situation. While I was still in the living room, wondering what would happen next.

I was just fourteen back then, and seeing my grandmother and my dad go up against each other with their guns was not something that was normal for me. I was terrified of the outcome. The baffling thing was that my mom still didn't leave Dad for good. I couldn't imagine how she could live with a guy who pulled out a gun on her mother. True, Mom Mom pulled out a gun on him first, but she did that to protect Mom. Still, my mother went back to him, even though living with him was only ruining her and my lives. As I was getting older, all those questions stayed with me, and I couldn't fathom why my mother dealt with all the mess she was stuck in due to Dad.

Dealing with such intense stuff at home, I kept it all a secret from the people who knew me at high school. I didn't want them to find out about the abuse, the beatings, or even that gun incident. So, I kept myself busy with sports and girls, embracing the persona of a confident and athletic young boy at high school.

I wanted to try out for the basketball team the first thing when I got into high school. I could have tried out for the Varsity squad, but they had rounded up a great team that year, and I knew that even though I would have made it through the selections, I would be sitting out on the bench in the games. So, I tried out for junior varsity instead, where I would get more opportunities to shine and get selected.

Just like my expectations, I quickly became the star player of the JV. The games gave me exposure and popularity, introducing me to the world of fleeting fame and fans. In high school, nobody ever messed with me because I could hold my ground and was the MVP of the basketball team.

I was the lead scorer on my high school basketball team and the best player, so of course, people admired my skills, and girls had crushes on me. I recall a beautiful junior-year student who was then dating the star of our school's varsity basketball team. However, she liked me, and I had the advantage of taking a senior player's girl from him based on my good looks and stellar performance in basketball. At that time, I already had my girlfriend, and this senior player's girl was also interested in hanging out with me, which made my homies jealous because I kind of had two girls at the same time.

I hated high school otherwise and was not interested in anything other than participating in sports and meeting new people. As I was the only boy from my project who had attended high school, I did not know any of my schoolmates except a few. So, I had to meet new people and form bonds with them, which I greatly enjoyed as I have always been a people person. I was very talkative and into people politics. So, I enjoyed befriending people and being in good company. So, high school was when I got to meet many new people, both younger and older than me, and it was also the time I built up my social confidence. I made new friends there, as most of my friends from the project joined high school in the later years.

Ninth grade was the best out of all four years I spent in high school. Playing for the Junior Varsity, I had been exposed to the limelight of winning games, being cheered on the court, and being surrounded by pretty girls. We won a few games that year and could have won more if we all worked together as a team—a unit that couldn't be toppled over. However, back in the day, we were all young and talented and wanted the spotlight to remain on us for as long as possible. We might not have been great at teamwork, but we displayed our skills and scored hard. Playing for the JV allowed me to meet several girls as well. Our home games were always packed, and I tried my best to look good whenever we went out to play. I always had a job and side hustles, so I saved enough money to wear polos, Air Max 91s, and all the cool stuff back in my day. I always had a fresh haircut and kept my appearance top-notch. That was one of the reasons I was not only a star on the basketball court but also a star with my admirers.

Back then, my older brother from Dad's first wife came to live with us for a few months because he was on the run. He eventually got locked up and went to the juvenile detention center Sleighton Farm when I was in the 9th grade and playing for the JV basketball team. After that, I met him during a basketball game in 1991 in high school.

We were playing for opposite teams, as he was representing Sleighton Farm. It was the only basketball game I got to play with him, and we were fully competing against each other. We had a great game as I scored 21 points and my brother scored 23 points, getting the win. We battled like we were not even brothers on the court and got a tech from the ref because he thought we were serious. We told him it was no big deal as we were brothers and were going head-to-head for the game.

My father didn't make it because he said he had to work and couldn't get access to town in time. He never came to watch me play, but I thought perhaps he would be there when both of us were playing. But my frail hope shattered when my eyes scanned the crowds and couldn't find him. As usual, he didn't bother showing up. He was probably on the streets, getting high and hanging out aimlessly.

Another experience that I can tie back to my high school days was the first time I smoked weed. By then, most of my friends from the project and the school were smoking weed already, but I steered clear of it because I was an athlete. I didn't want it to mess up with my system, and I certainly didn't want to become an addict like my dad.

So, I stayed away from weed and drugs. The only contact I had with drugs was selling them to make some extra money to support myself. I never smoked, got high, or did anything that would put me under the influence. In a sense, I had learned my lesson from seeing how my father's life turned out for him, so I made sure not to go down that route.

One day, I was hanging out with my best friend when I felt quite exhausted by everything around me. He was smoking weed at that moment, and I asked him to let me try. He refused, saying that I was going to get chosen for the NBA, so I should stay off drugs, even weed. I kept pestering him until he gave in and let me smoke a joint. It was a mirror image of how my dad asked his friend to let him try heroin, and he refused before ultimately giving in. I took that joint and smoked, but for the first time, I didn't feel anything.

I had always imagined that getting high was a feeling that made you lightheaded and forget all your worries. But for the time being, I did not feel anything of the sort. So, the next time I smoked weed, I did it for longer until I could feel that heady sensation take hold of me. But aside from weed, I never got involved with drugs or alcohol. I knew it was bad for my health and could affect my career as an athlete, so I kept myself in check.

Unlike my dad, I didn't succumb to the addiction to drugs and intoxication. My father didn't have a house, he paid no bills, and he lived a carefree life, running away from responsibility. I didn't want to end up like him, so I vowed to avoid everything else that could mark my fate similarly.

Despite the abuse and the rough life at home, I didn't let it cloud people's perception of me in high school. Outside the confines of my house, I soared high like a bird, gliding through the clouds of success and recognition. I was an athlete, a basketball player, and a well-liked boy from my class. Thus, I didn't let my self-esteem plummet just because my life at home was worse.

However, I had a lot of nervous energy at home, making me almost burst at the seams. Mom and Dad's constant fights kept me on edge, combined with Dad's anger that he often showered on me. I was caught up in a tangled web of emotions at home, between wanting to run away from that life and still feeling a tether binding me to those four walls.

Perhaps that was exactly why my mother didn't leave him even after everything he did and said to her. She could have felt the same way as I did for a point, thinking that our family would eventually pull through this mess. Thus, eight years lapsed in her marriage to Dad, yet he did not change. He stayed carefree and reckless despite the time that passed, making my mom realize that living with him any longer would be a lost cause. I was the fifth oldest of his kids, and after me, he had three kids from different women. His life was simply a pendulum of going back and forth between women, old habits, drugs, and recklessness. When my mom left my dad, they got divorced, and my dad eventually got married to his last wife. But he didn't have any more children after that. We were all grown by that time.

Seeing him juggle all those problems that complicated his life was an eye-opener for me. All his chaotic life choices solidified my own resolve to craft a life that would nowhere near reflect the life he lived. The contrast between my high school success and tumultuous home life became a burning motivation. It fueled my determination to break free and build a life of stability and love, far from the wreckage my father left behind. The bird that soared in high school has flown even higher, forever grateful for the escape those wings provided.

While the scars of my childhood remain, they also serve as a constant reminder of my resilience and the importance of building a life filled with love, support, and stability—the very things that were missing at home.

Chapter 7

Throughout my life, I met many people who impacted me in both good and bad ways. I remember when I was younger, I was close with Tommy, an older guy who was a friend of my mom. He took me under his wing and looked out for me the best he could. I hold fond memories of my time with him as he was the one who taught me a lot without having to drill it in me, unlike my dad.

He took me to get my first bank account, got me a MAC card, and used to help me with my homework. He was like an elder brother to me, and I looked up to him a lot. Tommy took me swimming and would go with me to buy hoagies. Thus, I had a memorable time with him, and he was one of the few people who inspired me to do good and be there for others.

Another positive influence who was almost like a father figure to me was Mr. Johnson. He was my basketball coach in high school and quickly gained a special place in my heart. He coached me until tenth grade, and I learned a lot about the game and practical life from him. We are still on great terms today, and he lives close to me, about twenty-five minutes away from my house.

Aside from the men in my life who turned out to be my mentors, I also learned a lot on the streets of the project, where I spent my childhood and made my first few friends. It was also where I was first introduced to sports, and I saw that they served as an excellent outlet for all the energy that bustled in me. I started playing with my friends in the project even before high school, and I discovered my love for sports there. We played tackle football on the pavement and the grass, and we also played basketball and baseball. I even won the championship for the Olney Eagles, which I consider one of my proudest moments.

However, how I started playing basketball and getting involved with the game is also a rather interesting story. I might never have expected how one swapping of places with my friend opened up a door to the most eventful chapter of my life.

When I was in fifth grade, I made a friend outside of my project who played basketball for the Tabor Rams while I was playing football for the Olney Eagles. We became best friends and did everything together. My mom was his mom, and vice versa, and my dad was also nice to him. Through him, I went to play a basketball game for the Tabor Rams while he came to my project and played football with us. Thus, I was introduced to basketball and realized my love and passion for it. I was ten or eleven years old when I learned to play basketball and shoot accurately. I was the better basketball player, and he was the better football player.

Football was my main sport growing up and was my first love as I enjoyed the man it made out of me. But when I started loving basketball, I had to work hard to prove I was worthy of the court. I practiced and learned how to shoot, investing hours of struggle into my basketball skills. But all my efforts paid off in the end, as I improved my game remarkably. I loved basketball because of the competition, and I was a great shooter and defender. Basketball saved my life as it gave me an outlet to expel all the negativity and anger that built up as a result of my father's treatment at home. Once I really figured out that this was a sport I was going to excel in, it took me away from everything. When I was playing on the court, I had no bad thoughts, no negativity, and only the adrenaline pumping through my veins fueled me to go for the win.

In short, if I hadn't played basketball and ended up loving the sport, I don't think I would have made it this far. I don't think I would even be living, or I might be in jail somewhere. Thus, basketball became my lifeline, pulling me out of the rough waters in which my life was constantly circling.

I always had a job or side hustle to pay for my expenses, so I ensured that I had a fresh haircut, good clothes, and shoes to keep up with the image I created. Thus, my ninth grade flew by rather pleasantly, and even though things at home were tough, I always held my head high.

The phrase *chin up* seemed a perfect representation of my resilience because I maintained a tough front in high school no matter what I went through at home.

Despite everything I went through at home, I kept my school life separate and enjoyed my time the most I could. I always thought highly of myself and never let my dad's treatment affect me to the point that I would start doubting my worth. A lot of people would have crumbled under the pressure—some could have even ended their lives. But I stood my ground and resiliently made it through the difficult phases of my life.

In high school, I wasn't as tall as the rest of the guys who played basketball, being only 5'10", but I made up for my height with my offensive shooting skills. My defense was great, too, and it, all in all, made me a force to be reckoned with on the court.

Thus, I was always a standout player. My love for basketball offered me an opportunity to channel all my frustration and energy into the sport. I was good at playing both offensive and defensive. My friends and I used to play both basketball and football, but I was the only one of them who played baseball. I played baseball for a Catholic school and was quite well-rounded at the game. My attitude toward every sport was that once I started playing it, I simply had to get good at it. So, I would practice for hours until I achieved the excellence I wanted. We also played baseball with my older brother for Moreland, now known as the Hank Gathers Center.

From a young age, I knew I had the charm and the looks that made girls admire me. Influenced by my dad's words that we were handsome dudes who need not worry about pickup lines to get together with the ladies, I got involved with girls very young. So, from junior high to high school, I had always been a ladies' man and could date any girl I wanted to. I started having sex quite young, when I was probably in third or fourth grade. From then onwards, it became a welcome respite to surround myself with people, mess around with the beautiful girls, and play basketball, which had become second nature to me.

In high school, I played for the junior varsity team, and then I also played for a recreation team. I had a basketball game in high school at 3:30, and then, at night, I had another game with the recreation team. So, I invested my whole life in the sport and improved my skills with every passing day. When I was on that basketball court, I was just locked in on the present moment, and the rest of the world didn't even matter. I enjoyed what I did, and it got me through everything.

I not only played the game but also watched and studied it thoroughly. Basketball was undoubtedly a huge part of my life in high school and beyond. It kept me away from everything that could have ruined me and set me on a path to self-destruction. I didn't loiter on the streets and never got caught up with the wrong crowd because I was investing my efforts in my game. Even in my roughest and darkest times, basketball was a guiding light and the only thing I could look forward to. It got me through the tempests of my life, and even today, I feel grateful that I found my true calling in the sport and that it impacted me positively.

The only downside of having a great first year in high school was that it inflated my ego and made me think I could take on anything and everything. Fate proved me wrong multiple times after that, and I couldn't play basketball for the first half of the season in tenth grade but came back during the playoffs. As my first report card came out, I was told to sit on the bench for the high school games. I was still playing for a travel team, but it didn't give me the same thrill, and I longed to return to my high school's basketball court.

Playing Basketball for the Travel Team

In the meantime, I worked diligently to maintain my grades in high school and played in another league. When my second report card came, and I had improved considerably, I got a spot on the Varsity squad. I was over the moon, and I knew it was my time to shine and show my skills.

However, back in the 90s, it was a tough and competitive environment for basketball and other professional sports in Philadelphia. Only a few people got to clear all the obstacles to become professional players. While I had the chance to show my skills and be scouted by a good college for their team, I also knew the competition was very tough. I hadn't played in that ruthless environment for a few months, as things were rather different in the other league that I played for. But as I had returned, I decided to work hard, practice, and gain back my position as the star player.

I remember playing against one of the best teams in Philadelphia and hoping that I would perform my best and get scouted. That game was one of the toughest I had faced, and even though I knew we stood no chance of winning, I was determined to give my best. My team lost that game, giving me a taste of what it felt like to lose on the court but still hold my head high. Other than that basketball game, my tenth grade in high school was the same pendulum of basketball, girls, and money. But it wasn't as stellar as the ninth grade.

I was getting older, and several new experiences awaited me, so I didn't let the thought of having a bad tenth grade deter me. I was determined to make the best out of that situation and prove my worth, nevertheless.

Fels High Varsity Squad

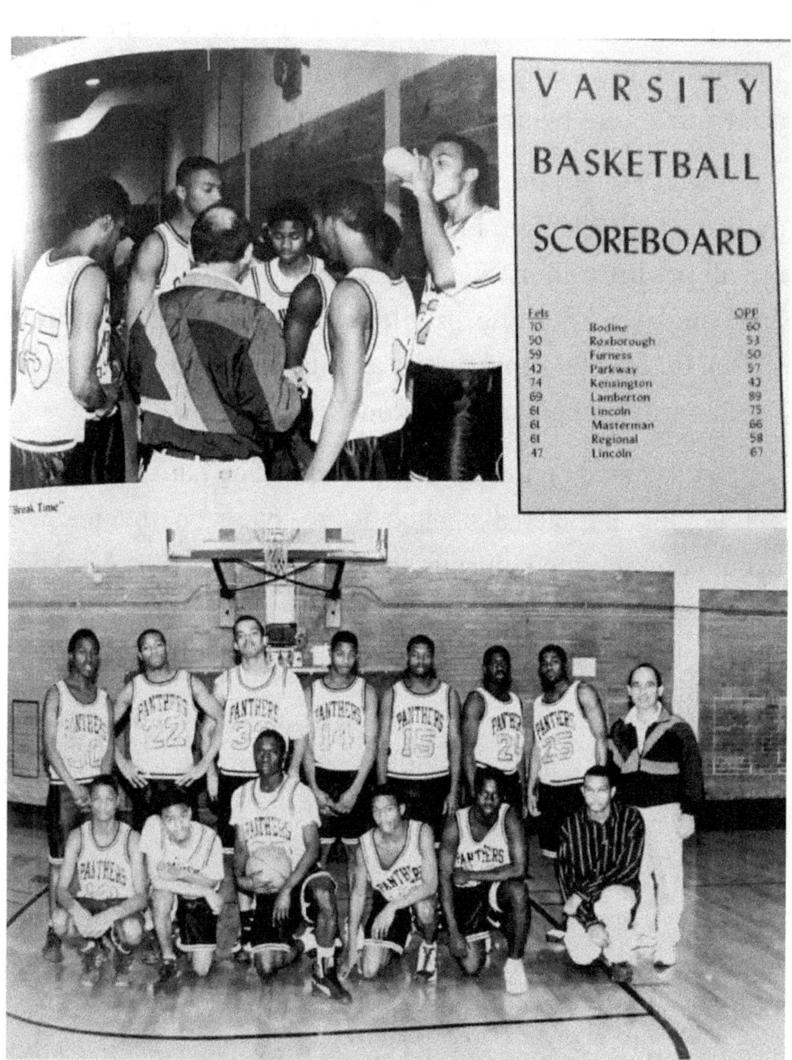

Varsity Basketball Team

Chapter 8

During tenth grade, in the first half of the basketball season, my grades dropped. I could not concentrate on my studies and wasn't allowed to play either because my academics were being affected by the sport.

It was a tough time for me as I lost the only escape I had to distract myself from my abusive personal life and channel out all the frustration from my system. I knew I had to work hard and win back the privilege of representing my high school on the basketball team, and the first thing I had to do for that was to maintain my grades.

So, I stayed on the bench while working hard to improve my grades and get a chance to be back on the team. I eventually rejoined during the playoffs when my grades improved.

Life at home was not much different either, although I got to see my dad rarely as he was busy with his two jobs. Sometimes, he would stay out the whole day and return late at night. However, I was no longer afraid of him and felt that I was old enough to take him on.

By the end of the basketball season, my grades dropped again slightly, and Mom found out that I was messing around in high school, so she told Dad to ask me about my studies. Like every other parent, she wanted my dad to give me a reality check so that I could go back to performing well in academics along with basketball. However, it backfired as my dad didn't take it well and got very angry. I was surprised to see him at home that day as he was usually busy with his jobs or hanging out with his friends. Standing in the doorway, I saw him with a Louisville Slugger bat in his hand and a frown on his face.

He started talking to me in his rough voice, asking me why I was bullshitting in school. He said that Mom told him I was not paying attention to my studies. "Why are you effing up in school? What's going on?"

I knew it would only escalate from there when he started swinging the bat, and I took a step back. The bat he was holding was metallic, and it was broken from the edge, so it could stab worse when used to hit someone.

My dad hit me on the arm with the bat, swinging it hard enough that the broken edge caught onto my skin. It agitated me, and I asked, "What are you doing? Don't hit me with that bat no more." I was getting mad at him, but he swung again, hitting my arm in the same spot.

From then onward, the argument turned into a volley of sermons as he started yelling at me and hitting the bat on the top of the door out of anger. He thought it would scare me, and he kept hitting the door, but I was also losing my calm by then. He struck me twice even though I didn't do anything to him. But the worst happened when the bat slipped from his hand as he was hitting the top of the door and slid down, hitting me in the face. It wasn't intentional, but I got badly injured, unable to assess where the pain was coming from. All I could see was red, and I shouted, making both my parents nervous. I thought my nose was broken, so I rushed to the bathroom to check and saw that my forehead was cut open, blood tricking down from the deep gash.

I had to be taken to the hospital, and my dad told me he didn't mean to bust open my head with the bat. It slipped from his hand and struck me. Stopping the bleeding, my mother took me to the hospital, where I got six stitches to seal that wound.

If I told the hospital staff how I got that cut, my dad would have been locked up, so he asked me to lie and tell them that I fell and busted my head as a result. I had to lie then to protect my father even though I did not want to. Intentional or not, he had hit me twice in the arm with that bat already. That strike on the head was the last straw. He didn't even come with Mom to take me to the hospital.

After that accident, my dad stopped hitting me. It seemed to have scared him and put things into perspective for him that if I got hurt worse, he could get locked up. Even though he still got angry at me and yelled at me, he stopped physically abusing me.

Thus, that accident was a transition in my life when I became more than just a child getting beaten up by his dad. I knew I could take him on if he ever hit me again, and I had the confidence to stand up for myself and my mom.

Back in seventh grade, I had tried standing up to him once when he was yelling at me for eating his cookies. He had kept some cookies in the refrigerator, which I ate, and it made him angry. I vividly recall thinking I had had enough of the shouting and I could take him on. So, I threw my hat on the ground and puffed up my chest, making myself seem bigger to counter him. However, he had punched me in the chest so hard that I felt I wouldn't be able to breathe again.

Fast forward to tenth grade when I got hit by the bat, but I didn't back down, so I told him to stop. He didn't intentionally strike me in the face with the bat, but it happened and made him realize that he was at fault. From then onward, I decided to face his anger head-on and stand up for myself instead of taking the beating.

Tenth grade ended, and eleventh began, though it was also not a very remarkable year for me. The past year, I worked hard on my grades and was allowed to play varsity basketball with my high school team again. I knew then that I had another chance to dive into the sport I loved and leave my mark on the court. I only kept coming to high school to keep my grades up, play basketball, and spend my free time with girls. Other than that, I was occupied with my jobs and side hustles, working hard to earn every penny.

My home life was the same without the physical abuse. It only became more mental abuse as my dad would say whatever came to mind and vent out his anger through words. But it wasn't frightening anymore because I was a grown man myself and could stand my ground against him.

He would come home late, just like my mom, as she started working more hours at the hospital. Sometimes, Dad came home after his first job ended to rest and then left for his second job. Otherwise, he spent his free time with his friends and went to work directly without coming home in between. Thus, our contact lessened, but he was still a huge part of my life that I couldn't possibly ignore.

One day, he and my mother got into an argument while I was at home. My dad worked himself up in quite a state, and my mom was also yelling at him. It was almost a routine for me and my siblings to watch our home shake with the impact of all that shouting and yelling. By then, we should have gotten accustomed to it.

However, when my dad tried to hurt Mom, or at least I thought he was going to hurt her, I came in between. I had never interfered in their arguments before, but right then, I had had enough.

I told him then firmly, "If you put your hands on my mom again, I will make you pay."

I grabbed the bat he hit me with and held it threateningly to make him stop. I probably would have smacked him with it if not for my mom, who made me cool down.

But after that, it was crystal clear to Dad that I had grown from the young Wayne who put up with all of his beatings and abuse. He could see that I had emerged stronger from all the hardships I faced and would stand as a firm protector for my mom and myself.

Chapter 9

During my eleventh grade, I came off the bench to play for the Varsity Squad. By then, I was attending high school and maintaining my grades just so I could play sports. We had a good team, and one of my seniors, a White boy named Joe, was really good at the game. He was tall and could shoot the ball very well.

I used to watch him play and wanted to be better than him. Since basketball was my love, it was my unspoken passion to do my best and be the best player out there.

Once my dad found out about Joe, he told me that I simply had to beat him. He motivated me to up my game and set him down. He kept saying that I had to score on him, and I did it, which ended up in my favor as he fell off the team later that year while I kept playing.

Basketball became my sanctuary and the only good part of my life in eleventh grade at high school. Other than that, I was still involved in my hustles, making money by selling weed. I didn't do drugs in high school, but I smoked weed. I grew up with a dad on drugs and knew the consequences if I gave in to that addiction, so I always steered clear of anything other than weed.

Home was still the same for me, but it was no longer as frightening because my dad stopped hitting me. He still kept up with the mental and verbal abuse, calling me a motherfucker and tearing me down with his words. But at least the physical abuse had come to an end. Then, I started twelfth grade and was still playing on the team. While the last year in high school was supposed to be easy for most students, I made it hard on myself by not really paying attention to my studies. Basketball had my full attention, and when my dad offered me the opportunity to play in a tournament with prison inmates, I agreed.

So, twelfth grade marks another milestone as I played on the team that went up to Graterford Prison in Pennsylvania. It was a prison facility up in the mountains, and a team comprising the best basketball players in Philly was going up to play a tournament with the inmates.

It was an opportunity that I didn't hesitate to take, and soon enough, I trained with all the other players who were just as good and sometimes better than me in basketball. Back in those days, the Simon Gratz basketball team in Philly had all the best players. One of my homies, Redz, was also on that team. We had known each other since before I went to high school, and I met him again while training for the tournament. He was a little older than me by maybe a year or two, but we played in the same public league basketball.

However, when it was time to go up to the prison to play the tournament, my homie Redz couldn't participate. He told me that he was going to La Salle University and he was going to be the starting point guard. So, playing in the tournament at Graterford would be a violation of college rules for him. We had to drop Redz out at the last moment, but we still took a great team up there to play at the tournament. All the players that were going to play against the inmates were the best in their form and were from my dad's friend Sam's team. Before going to the prison, we practiced with each other, and I got to play with some of the best players in Philly. It was a moment that I am proud of. It was a dream come true for a basketball enthusiast as I watched the game, played it, studied it, and even went to the live games. At times, it seemed my whole life revolved around basketball, and without it, I wouldn't have been able to get through all the challenges fate threw at me.

Finally, the day came for us to go to the Graterford prison. We were supposed to be there for an all-day tournament, and it was my first time stepping into a prison facility. My dad got a chance to meet his friends, whom he hadn't seen in a long time, as they were in prison, so he came along with me. He used to be in a gang, so a lot of his gang guys were there in jail.

Before the game started, our team players were given wristbands in one color to differentiate us from the inmates' team, who also had wristbands but in a separate color. Two guards with guns in their hands were keeping watch while the rest of the ground was full of inmates who had come to watch the game. I thought that if the inmates wanted to take us hostage, they could easily do so because we were outnumbered heavily. But nothing of the sort happened, and the inmates were all cool with us. One of the inmates tried to intimidate me because I was younger than the rest of the guys on the team. So, he approached me and told me that I should swap my wristband with him. If he had my wristband, he would be able to walk free from the prison. I refused, knowing the repercussions. Then the tournament started, and we played our first game against them, which ended up really good. We played three games in the tournament and won the first game.

Our team was beating the other team, but the inmates never ran out of players, and whenever any player of theirs got tired, they subbed in new players. After every couple of minutes, they would sub-players, so they had an advantage over us as all our players were getting tired. We lost because they had more men than us. We played the third game and won, and I had a very good game, hitting a lot of 3-pointers.

I remember that tournament for many reasons. It was my first and last time being in a prison facility. I will never forget that weekend as it was a great experience for me. We played a good game but got tired as we didn't have many players to sub in. Still, we did our best, and I played with the best players on my team.

But being in jail for that short time made me realize that I didn't want to end up in prison like the countless people who had come to watch the game and were playing against us. While we were there, nothing out of order happened, but I knew it was a dreary place with all those men locked up like animals for the crimes they committed. Some of the inmates were even innocent men locked up for crimes they didn't commit but couldn't prove their innocence. There were no women in jail, and just all the guys locked up. That day, I vowed never to do anything that would get me sentenced. I wouldn't mind going to another tournament, but I never wanted to go to jail.

However, I once got involved in a fight that escalated to such an extent that the whole project watched. Anyone living in my project could tell you what a fight it was and how everyone was gathered to see the outcome. Even though I tried to stay away from trouble, this was the biggest fight I had been in.

It had been a sunny day, and I was relaxing at home, dressed in my fresh clothes—my Chuck Taylors, Nautica shorts, and a nice polo shirt. I always looked fly and dressed my best. That day, I was waiting to meet a girl, so I took my polo off. The next thing I knew, there was a knock at the door, and I was told that a guy had hit my sister. I rushed outside and saw my sister arguing with him. She said he owed her money from a card game down at the park. I tried to calm the situation, but my sister kept pushing him, getting right in his face.

The guy she was arguing with was known for beating people in the project. He would body slam people and do crazy stuff, so no one really messed with him. He used to wrestle, and he even beat the guy who I once got into a fight with over slapboxing. But I had never gotten into trouble with him earlier because we were cool with each other. While I was listening to his side of the story, my sister left. Suddenly, she came back with a big butcher knife, demanding he give her the money. I quickly intervened, taking the knife from her. As I was taking it inside, the crowd that had gathered started yelling, "He hit your sister! He hit your sister!"

I knew the truth—he was just trying to push her off him—but with all those people around, I couldn't back off, or it would make me look like a punk. I had to hold my own and not look like a bitch in front of anybody. So I walked over to him and said, "Bro, did I say you don't hit my sister?"

That was when the fight broke out. I knew what he would do because I had seen him use his moves; we grew up together, and I was prepared for what he had in store for me. He tried to grab and slam me, using those crazy wrestling moves he was known for. We traded blows, slamming each other to the ground, and he grabbed my balls. I was hitting him with everything I had, even headbutting him, but he wouldn't let go. Then, my sister stepped in and stomped him in the head, allowing me to break free.

He took off running, and we headed back inside the house. But about thirty minutes later, there was a commotion outside—that guy, his sister, and some other dudes armed with bats, chains, and pipes gathered outside our house, waiting to get back on us. My dad was asleep back then but woke up from all the noise and came out. My sister told him that the guy owed her money, and because he hit her, a fight broke out between me and him. Now, my dad was from North Philly and not to be messed with, so he came out of the house and said some wild shit that totally threw them off.

Seeing the guy who I was in a fight with, he said, "The fuck wrong with y'all, coming to my fucking house with this bullshit? Boy, I fuck niggas like you in jail." He walked them all the way back down the long pathway from our house. But the guy said, "Mr. Nick, I just want to fight Wayne one-on-one."

Dad told me, "Wayne, come and fight this nigga, he wants to rumble."

I couldn't back down like a coward. My dad had prepared me for that moment ever since I was eleven. I did not take all those ass-whoopings for nothing. So, the next thing I knew, I went back outside, tied up my Chucks, and was ready to throw him down.

The whole neighborhood was out, forming a big circle around us. This happened before social media was available, so our fight was like a live entertainment channel for most people. I was thinking, *"Wayne, you better not get fucked up. You've been getting your ass whooped. Your pop is showing you how to rumble."*

I knew he was crazy and had beaten a lot of dudes' asses, but he wasn't gonna beat my ass. So, there we go, we start rumbling and getting it in. I got some good shots in, and he got some good shots in. It was a fair fight because I knew my sister started all the trouble, so if one of us fell, the other let him get up. In the end, nobody really got the upper hand; the fight ended in a tie, and we just went our separate ways. My dad told me he was proud of me. He said I stood my own ground and proved that he made me strong enough not to get beaten badly. A few days later, I was still sore from the fight, with some scratches and a chipped tooth. When I look in the mirror today, I still see the chip in my tooth, reminding me of that time.

But that guy and I moved on from that incident. That guy and I were already cool with each other, but I earned his respect that day. We crossed paths once and just shook hands, laughing about the whole situation. Not long after that, I heard he and a few other guys got lifetime imprisonment for committing murder. It's crazy how things could escalate so quickly over nothing.

***

Another experience that I could never forget was prom in twelfth grade. I was eighteen then, and initially, I didn't want to go because I failed my driving test and didn't get my license. But a girl wanted to take me as her date, and she had a car, so I ended up going with her. But on the way to prom, we got into an accident.

I banged my head hard on the dashboard, but we were still able to drive the car up to prom. It was in a terrible condition after the accident, but we ended up enjoying the night. I felt like a grown man who had his life sorted out and could sit back and relax with his homies, dancing to the music and having nothing to worry about. Prom was one of the few things in my final year that I ended up enjoying to the fullest.

Prom Night with Me and My Parents

Me at Senior Year Prom

However, I didn't get to graduate with my classmates at the end of high school. I was so taken with basketball, playing tournaments, and basketball with the Varsity squad that I was only doing the bare minimum in my academics. So, I had to take a do-or-die test, but I only got 63 on it and failed. I needed two more points to get enough points to graduate. But I couldn't make it because I was not paying much attention to my studies. So, I had to attend summer school while all my peers graduated in June.

It was 1995, and I was one year behind my mates as I had to go to summer school. If I had graduated with them, I would have been celebrating and enjoying my life. But I was stuck in summer school, where I worked hard so that I could get my diploma.

The day I finally received my diploma and left high school was a big release from every stressful thing that was going on in my life. It felt like I had gained freedom and could soar high in the sky. Ever since childhood, I haven't let the bad parts of my life define me. Instead, I worked hard and built up my resilience to endure everything but still succeed.

Another surprise awaited me after I graduated high school. One of the girls I was messing around with back when I was in high school told me five or six months later that she was pregnant and it was my child. By then, I had a girlfriend from West Philly. I asked her how that happened because when we were together, she had told me she was on the pill, and believing her, I hadn't used a condom back then.

She told me that she lied about the pill earlier and was going to have my baby. Though at first, I didn't believe her. However, once my daughter was born, I knew she was my child. I was fresh out of high school when I became a dad at nineteen years old. It was the 27th of January 1996 when my daughter was born.

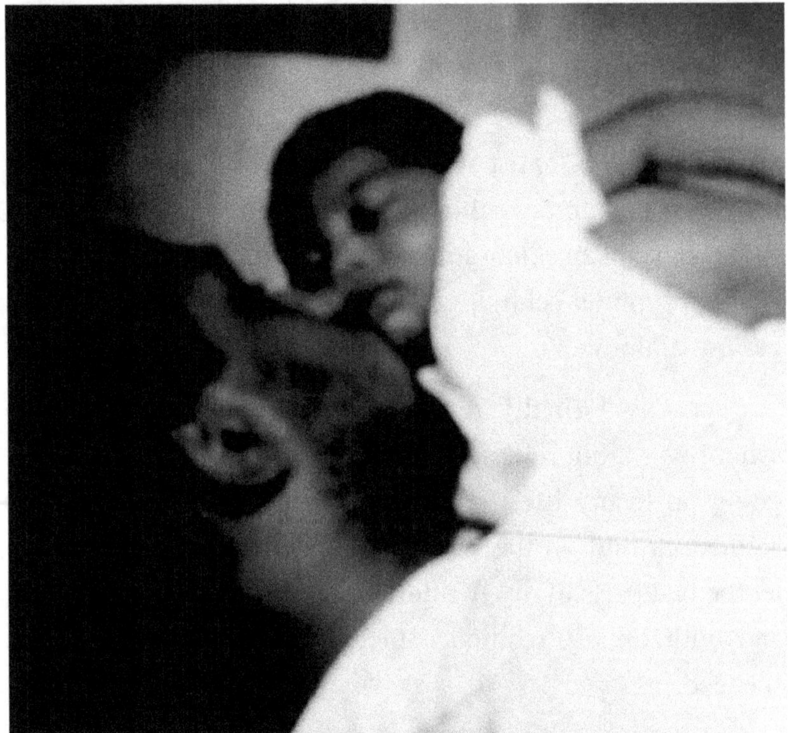

Me with My New-Born Daughter

My responsibilities increased, but I was determined to fulfill them all to the best of my ability. Everything that I had been through in my life, everything that my dad put me up to, was like a boot camp for me, teaching me how to survive. Growing up, I dealt with some of the worst things a boy has to go through, but it made me stronger and able to deal with life's challenges later on. From a young boy, I grew into an independent and strong person who did his best to help people but never let anyone walk over him. Thus, my character evolved positively after all my hardships, and I was able to make the best of my life.

I graduated high school, have a daughter, and have a better relationship with my father after all those years. Aside from basketball, Mom Mom was my strongest support as she always wanted to keep me safe and stood up for me. She was like a second mom to me, as she always had my back and made sure that I became strong and resilient. When I look back at my life, I feel a surge of pride. Despite all the terrible hands fate dealt me, I still turned the game in my favor and emerged victorious.

Me and My Daughter

Me and My Daughter

Me and My Mom Mom

With My Mom Mom

Chapter 10

Life after high school took me through a lot of ups and downs. But I was never one to falter in my path and kept going straight ahead, willing to fulfill all my dreams and be the best father to my daughter.

I was twenty back then, and I had mountains ahead of me to climb. My dream was to utilize my future by trying to get into a college and finish pursuing my passion for basketball. However, I didn't have the right people around me for guidance at the time when I needed them most.

After graduating high school, I was standing at a crucial threshold of my life—a transition from a carefree youth to a practical life full of responsibilities and hardships. However, I had never had it easy, even in my childhood, so I was well prepared to face the challenges waiting for me.

My mom didn't push college on me because she thought I didn't like studying and was only maintaining my grades to keep playing basketball. As soon as I was out of high school, she told me to get a job so I could be able to support myself.

Thus, I ended up getting a job instead of pursuing basketball as a career or going to college. I was looking at the circumstances around me, knowing that I was a young father with responsibilities. It would be better if I had a stable job through which I could generate a better income for my family. I was still young and thrust into the responsibility of being a father to a newborn girl. Throughout the way, I was learning how to be a good father to her and making sure that she had the best of everything I could give her. My personal experiences made me want to do better with my life and provide much more to my girl, including emotional support and love.

Being a loving father to my daughter wasn't difficult, but things were slightly strained between me and the baby mom. But I pushed myself forward, thinking that it wasn't just about me anymore. Now, I had a daughter, and my ex was an important part of my child's life, being her mother. So, I didn't let my issues with the baby mom keep me from seeing and caring for my daughter. In fact, the biggest motivation I had to find a job and earn well was so I could provide for my daughter.

Me and <u>My Daughter</u>

I was still living with my mom back then; we moved from the projects down to North Philly, Wyoming Ave. We had a mixed population on D & Wyoming, including Asians, African Americans, and Hispanic people. Accustomed to having a job, I kept myself busy there as well, and when I didn't have anything to do, I always found a side hustle to generate money. My daughter was living with her mother back then, but I had no restrictions on bringing her to my home. So, she stayed with us, too, and went back and forth between me and her mom.

While we were living on D & Wyoming, I clashed a lot with my mom. I didn't know if she got bitter after all those years of tolerating my father or if it was because of my sister, who used to tell on me a lot and had a problem with me. But my mom and I got into a lot of arguments, so by 1999, I moved into my apartment in East Oak Lane in the lower suburbs with my girlfriend and soon-to-be son's mother. We met in 1997 after my daughter's mom and I broke up. My daughter was a year old by then.

At that point, I felt that life was finally taking a turn toward brighter paths. I was young and trying to make it in life with my own little apartment and my car. I bought a used car when I moved out of my mom's place, and she helped me get it by putting it in her name. However, I paid for the car with the money I saved and was able to buy it. I felt the rocky slopes of my life finally straighten into a track I wanted to tread on.

As I was living on my own, I found a job at a furniture company through a temp agency. But I had to leave that job as it was temporary. By then, two months had passed with me living on my own, I had new bills to pay, and with the lack of money, things were starting to turn bleak again.

My girlfriend was working at that time, too, and I was trying to figure out how to get another job and generate a stable income. Things came to the point that I was ready to pawn some of my jewelry to get money to pay for the expenses. However, the temp agency I worked for contacted me and told me they had a job downtown at Comcast. They said it was a one-day job, and I turned down that offer because I wanted something more sustaining than working for one day. Two days in a row, I refused their offer, but having no other means to pay my bills, I finally decided to go to Comcast and took the job.

In 1999, Comcast didn't have its own building and only had a few floors in another building. So, I reported there for my temporary job, and they asked me to move some boxes out of the storage closets. They were arranging a Christmas party and wanted to have more space. I did what was asked of me and didn't find it hard because I had worked in warehouses and was used to moving heavy stuff around.

By the time I got home that day, the agency called me and told me that even though they had initially offered only a one-day job, the people at the company wanted me to work with them for the rest of the year. Perhaps they chose to hire me because of my personality, the way I dressed, or my work ethic. Thus, I got a job at Comcast and started immediately. It was like a sign from God that, *"Wayne, you just got to do it, man."*

I took the job and started working in the mail room, getting paid good money for delivering mail. I could pay my bills, and things were back on track. As time passed, I got on good terms with a lot of my colleagues. I was particularly popular with the ladies. As I said earlier, I was a ladies' man.

Even though I was just there doing my job, I didn't mind the company of my female colleagues, and they liked to hang out with me, too.

However, this popularity at work came with its downsides. One of the older guys, a permanent employee, felt that I was a threat to him. He worked there before me, and he thought he was the ladies' man until the real ladies' man came to work there.

He didn't like me getting all the attention, so he went to the HR lady and lied about me. She called me into the office, but his attempt to get me fired didn't work, though it made me more cautious.

It made me nervous sometimes because I thought I would lose my job due to him. He was permanent, and I was just a guy hired for a temporary job. So even though I was pissed off at him, I couldn't say anything to him.

I worked there till the Christmas Party, but after that, it was all over. The head of Human Resources at HR told me that he would get me an interview and that I could get hired permanently at the company, but I hadn't heard from him for a long time. I kept calling him but got no response.

My girlfriend got pregnant with my son before I was permanently hired at Comcast. I remember right after she had our son in 2000, I had to go back to our apartment to get her some clothes and saw an eviction notice on our door. My emotions were all over the place because I just had a newborn son, but we could get kicked out in the street.

Things turned hard again, and I was broke, sitting in the lobby for hours and waiting to be called up. Often, I got messages from the head of HR to come talk to him, and then I would wait in the lobby for hours until he sent someone saying that he couldn't meet me and that I must come another day. It was the worst feeling to cling to hope and watch others trample over it intentionally.

I felt devastated and defeated. But all my patience paid off, and a month later, in February 2000, I finally got an interview with Comcast in the northeast of Philadelphia. I got hired on the spot and stayed with the company for ten years. I could pay my bills and support my family, making me think that things were finally stable for us after a period of obstacles in our path.

By then, my girlfriend and I got engaged, and it felt like a positive step in the right direction back then. My daughter also came to visit me for the weekends, and I found my personal heaven in my apartment, surrounded by the people I loved.

Me, My Son, and My Son's Mom

However, after five years of being together, my son's mom and I broke off our engagement in January 2003. As a couple, we couldn't make things work, so we chose to separate our ways. That really hurt because she took my son from me. I was used to seeing him every day but then went to see him only if I stopped over at her house or every other weekend. So, I was by myself and needed a fresh start. I thought of getting a new home and starting from scratch.

I was paid well at Comcast and made a lot of money working there. I was able to buy a new house in 2004 and could live a good life. I lived in that house for over eighteen years. Thus, when I left my job, I had a good severance package, a 401K, which I transferred over.

Thus, my personal life was set, and so was my career, as after working for ten years at Comcast, I worked again for the Post Office, then for Amazon, and for every big company out there. Currently, I am working at Amazon, which I thought was the best fit for me. I have been there for seven years.

Then, I met my wife in 2007. I met her and dated her for a year, after which we got engaged. Then, we decided to get married in 2009, and we have been together ever since.

My Wife and I At Our Wedding

When I got laid off from the company, I had my own comedy shows going on every month. I made a lot of money by creating my own comedy production, becoming the biggest promoter in Philly between 2009 and 2014.

I sold my house in 2020, and we bought a new home in 2021 in the suburbs. I am forty-eight now and living a damn good life with the woman I love. My wife is a beautiful woman inside out, and I love her from the depths of my heart. We have been together for seventeen years and have been married for fifteen years. We always have each other's backs despite the challenges that have come in our lives. My daughter is twenty-eight, and my son is turn twenty-four. Thus, my family is proof that I made it in life and achieved my goals.

We take a lot of vacations and enjoy our time together. I am glad that I found someone I could share my life with, my wife and partner who understands me and loves me for who I am. I know I can't be perfect, but I try to be the best person for my family—the best husband and father.

Me and My Lovely Wife

Me and My Kids

My upbringing taught me a lot about fatherhood and how it impacts young children. Thus, I never put my kids through what I suffered. I was a disciplinary figure in their lives, but I never beat or abused them. I would talk the issue out with them and try to understand their perspective as well. I felt that having a friendly relationship with children and making them comfortable enough to share their feelings openly were the most important things.

Despite everything I went through, I didn't let go of my ambition to become somebody and make it in my life. I still deal with the ups and downs of my life, but I have gotten much better at it than I was in my childhood. From the age of eleven onwards, I had dealt with some of the hardest stuff a boy my age could face, but I made it through by focusing on the important parts of life.

All the physical, mental, and verbal abuse, the beatings, and the bullying couldn't pull me down as I kept myself sane by playing basketball, surrounding myself with good friends, and channeling my frustration through sports, finding a positive way to let it all out. If I hadn't done so, who knows, I could have ended up mentally disturbed, or I could even have committed suicide under the pressure of my life. But my mind was strong enough to stand through all the challenges and overcome the abuse.

Later in my life, I was able to make a documentary and speak about my past and the terrible experiences I went through. Speaking about my life and sharing my challenges so that others going through similar situations wouldn't feel alone made me feel a lot better. Then, I reconnected with my father in 2011, and he apologized for his behavior toward me. His addiction and his past experiences influenced him to treat me the way he did, and when he came clean about it all, I was able to forgive him. I couldn't forget my past and wasn't going to, but I forgave my dad because he apologized with sincerity.

That apology helped me rebuild a good relationship with him. After that, my dad spent more time with me than any of his kids. We went to basketball and baseball games and often went out for dinner. We also visited each other's house simply to chill and enjoy the company. It was like getting back the version of a dad I always wanted to share my life with.

We have been very close to each other since then. A few years ago, I threw him a surprise birthday party, and we talked every day until he died in January 2024.

One thing my dad kept telling me before he passed away was: "Wayne, you're a good dude. Don't ever change. You hear me! You're a good dude. Don't ever change!"

His last few years were an attempt to reconnect and rebuild his relationship with me, and because I could accept his apology, I contributed to his efforts as well. True, the past could not be erased, but we were able to achieve a better present through our reconciliation.

Me and My Dad

With My Dad

Now, I live my life on my terms and have no burdens weighing me down. I have a loving family; I have been successful and stand on top of the mountain of challenges strewn across my path. Despite all those challenges, I climbed out of the darkness and was victorious.

My Mom Mom used to say, "Wayne, what I love about you is that no matter what happens, you're going to be able to change the world. No matter if you fall or things ain't going right. You might bend, but you never break. I love how you bounce back from things. I love that about you."

So, I make sure that I always do that in my life. I could have easily quit, just given up, or even killed myself, anything. You take ten kids, about 11 years old, and put them through what I went through. From 11 to 19, I guarantee half of them wouldn't make it because you have to be mentally strong to be able to go through some stuff.

In this book, I have laid bare my past to you, readers. I hope that my story helps people who find themselves in similar situations. People who are going through physical, mental, and verbal abuse, or all of these at the same time, my heart goes out to you, and I want you to know that you are not alone. You are strong, and You have the ability to make it in life. You just have to trust yourself and keep moving forward.

The message I wanted to convey from the very beginning to the end of the book is that life isn't always perfect, and sometimes it is downright terrifying. But what matters most is your inner strength and resilience to face your battles head-on.

If I, Wayne De-Langè Morris, could do it, then so can you. I still deal with the past experiences that affected me, but at the end of the day, they make me who I am today. Despite all the hardships, here I am standing in front of you, my life written clearly on these pages as a testament to my resilience. And you, my friend, will also overcome your challenges sooner or later.

All we need is hope, trust in ourselves, a positive outlet to channel all our anger and frustration and make it productive, and people who would stand by us and give their love and support. However, in this formula for success, the most crucial element is the self.

You are the most important person who can change the course of your life. Believe in yourself, and you can also conquer your fears, emerging triumphant after years of endurance.

Me and My Mom

My Mom Mom and Dad

Me and My Dad

Me and My Mom

Me and My Wife

Me and My Wife

Me and My **Kids**

Me and My Lil Brother

Me, My Wife, My Son, Three Siblings, and Other Family Members

Me with My Wife—My Eternal Support